WHAT'S THE BIG DEAL ABOUT

For my sweet Dante, Allegra,
and Romy. For justice.
—R.S.

Dedicated with love to Mama Joyce
and Papa Joe Remenar, and for Kris, alw
—M.F.

PHILOMEL BOOKS
An imprint of Penguin Random House LLC, New York

First published in picture book format by Philomel Books,
an imprint of Penguin Random House LLC, 2017.

Chapter book first published in the United States of America
by Philomel Books, an imprint of Penguin Random House LLC, 2020.

Visit us online at penguinrandomhouse.com

LIBRARY OF CONGRESS CATALOGING-IN-PUBLICATION DATA IS AVAILABLE.

Manufactured in China by
RR Donnelley Asia Printing Solutions Ltd.

HC ISBN 9780593114902 / 10 9 8 7 6 5 4 3 2
PB ISBN 9780593114872 / 10 9 8 7 6 5 4 3 2

Chapter book edited by Talia Benamy. Original picture book edited by Jill Santopolo.
Design by Jennifer Chung. Text set in Adobe Jenson Pro.

The art was created in three stages: first, thumbnail sketches—many small sketches
created for each illustration emphasizing page design, visual narrative, and light
source; second, intermediate sketches—several sketches created to refine the design
of the book's characters and their environment, details, etc.; and third, the final
art, which was created with watercolor and pencil on sanded Arches
140 lb. cold press paper.

HAT'S THE BIG DEAL ABOUT

Freedom

written by **Ruby Shamir**
illustrated by **Matt Faulkner**

PHILOMEL BOOKS

LAND
OF THE FREE

You know that feeling you get when you can finally unbuckle your seat belt after a long trip in a cramped car? Or when the bell rings on the last day of school before summer vacation? Or when you see a wide open field that you can run through without worrying about traffic or cars? That's freedom.

There are lots of ways to be free in America. Here, you're free to dress the way you want, speak your mind, and choose the people you want to be friends with. There are also freedoms we enjoy all together as a country, like the freedom to decide on the rules and choose who's in charge.

In a big country with lots of different people, freedom doesn't mean you can do anything you want all the time. It's a free country, all right, but you aren't free to hurt people or steal their stuff or damage things that aren't yours. That means that the right to freedom comes with certain responsibilities—to take care of each other, treat people fairly, and make sure that everyone else can live in safety and enjoy their freedom too.

When we celebrate freedom in America

we usually do it on July 4th—America's birthday. What happened on that day? How did it shape the future of freedom in America? What's the big deal about freedom, anyway?

Every year on July 4th, we celebrate America's birthday with fireworks, picnics, parades, and barbecues. If you lined up the millions of hot dogs people in America eat on the 4th, they'd stretch all the way from New York to China and back!

HOW DID AMERICA BECOME A FREE COUNTRY?

Today's United States of America began as thirteen English colonies ruled by the king of England, who acted like a big bully. He told the colonists what to do and made them pay money, called taxes, to England. American colonists weren't allowed to vote for their leaders in England and try to change rules they didn't like. Over time, the colonists started to realize that this wasn't fair and that their voices should matter.

In the summer of 1776, Thomas Jefferson and other patriots decided to stand up to the bullying. Jefferson wrote the Declaration of Independence to announce America's freedom from British rule.

This declaration announced that "all men are created equal" and have the right to "Life, Liberty and the pursuit of Happiness" that can never be taken away. Back then, only a small group of people got to enjoy American freedom, because we had slavery here and only certain folks were allowed to vote. But people started to feel that they lived in the "land of the free," and these ideas inspired Americans with dreams of greater freedom.

Even though he wrote the words that inspired every struggle for freedom in America, Thomas Jefferson kept slaves. Robert Hemings, an enslaved fourteen-year-old boy, served Jefferson while he wrote the Declaration of Independence in Philadelphia in the summer of 1776.

July 4th became America's birthday because on that day, more than 240 years ago, we declared that America would be its own independent country. But first, American patriots would have to fight for our freedom in a long war called the American

Revolution to break free from England and create this new country.

One of the signers of the Declaration of Independence, John Hancock, wrote his name EXTRA BIG, supposedly so that the king of England could read it without wearing glasses. It's why today a person's signature is called a "John Hancock."

WHAT CHANGED AFTER THE REVOLUTION?

The Colonial army, as the patriots were known, fought hard and finally, in 1783, America was free! But it wasn't yet the America we know today—it was more like a jumble of states that couldn't agree on much. So in 1787 men representing each state held a Constitutional Convention meeting to write rules that would form something new: a national government that represented "We the People."

The Constitutional Convention took place during a very hot summer in Philadelphia in 1787, before air-conditioning was invented. Even worse, the founders locked the door and nailed the windows shut to keep their discussions secret. You can bet there was a lot of hot air in that room! For four long months these men—called delegates— talked, debated, argued, and finally agreed on a plan: our Constitution, which is the supreme law of the land. States then held their own conventions, where elected delegates voted to accept the new Constitution.

Our Constitution organizes our government, dividing it into three branches that balance each other. Voters elect members of the House of Representatives and the Senate, and together they form the United States Congress. These members

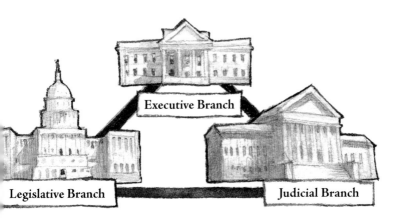

Executive Branch

Legislative Branch

Judicial Branch

of Congress pass the laws and make up the legislative branch. Voters also elect the president, who heads the executive branch and makes sure the laws are carried out and obeyed. The president also commands the military and leads our relations with other countries. Courts and judges make up the judicial branch, which settles arguments about the law and decides which laws the Constitution allows.

How many pennies are in a dollar? That's easy, right? One hundred! But in America's early days, states couldn't even agree on that. A dollar in New York wasn't worth the same amount as a dollar in Boston or in Philadelphia or in Charleston! The Constitution helped the states agree on rules and work together as a team.

WAS THE CONSTITUTION FINISHED RIGHT AWAY?

Our Constitution starts by stating that its mission is to make America "a more perfect Union," and as times change, we can change, or amend, the Constitution too. Early Americans didn't waste any time—they started amending the Constitution right away!

Before agreeing to accept, or ratify, the Constitution, people in many states worried that it would create a government that would be too powerful and might bully us again like the king of England had. So the founders promised to add a "Bill of Rights" to protect us.

While the Constitution says what the

government can do, the Bill of Rights—the first ten amendments to the Constitution—says that we the people have basic freedoms and rights that no government can take away. Thanks to the Bill of Rights, for example, our leaders can't send us to prison if we disagree with them or send police to search our homes just because they feel like it.

Together, the Constitution and the Bill of Rights say that the American people are in charge

and that our leaders get their power from us, which is very different from a king, who doesn't have to listen to anyone. When you can tell a bully to stop or go away, when you are in charge, the bully doesn't stand a chance.

The Bill of Rights keeps your freedom in balance with government power—like a seesaw. If you and a friend were riding up and down on a seesaw and your friend suddenly jumped off, you'd come crashing down with a thud! Both of you need to be on for the seesaw to work.

WHAT FREEDOMS DO WE GET FROM THE BILL OF RIGHTS?

The very first amendment of the Bill of Rights includes some of our most important freedoms. It says we have "freedom of speech"—the freedom to say whatever we want—and our leaders can't stop us, even if they don't like what we're saying. You even have the freedom to express your beliefs in school (just don't call out in class!).

Freedom of speech doesn't mean you can say anything you want at any time, especially if it hurts others. So you can't scream "fire!" in a crowded theater if there isn't really a fire, because folks might run out of the theater in a panic and hurt each other. And newspapers and magazines can't publish lies that they know aren't true and are meant to hurt people. Freedom of religion is another First Amendment right. It means you can go to any church, synagogue, mosque, or temple you want—or to none at all.

We also have freedom of the press, which means that journalists are free to investigate and write news reports on just about anything. There are still countries all over the world where people are thrown into jail for doing those things. But here, even kids are reporters and some have interviewed the president!

The First Amendment also says we're free to assemble. That means when you feel like your leaders aren't really listening, or the laws don't seem

fair, you can get together with friends and neighbors to try to make a change. How? By organizing marches or rallies or letter-writing campaigns to change people's minds or by convincing folks to vote for a new leader. And that's what our democracy is all about—the power of the people to set the rules and govern ourselves.

Have you ever noticed that people from different religions wear different kinds of head coverings? That's one of the ways we're free in America. And another way we're free is that we can go bareheaded if we choose!

DID THIS MEAN AMERICA WAS A PERFECTLY FREE COUNTRY?

Not quite.

The best way to protect "Life, Liberty and the pursuit of Happiness" for all Americans is to vote for our leaders—the people who make the laws. If the laws don't treat everyone fairly, voters are free to change our leaders, who then change the laws.

But the sad truth is, in early America most of the people who lived in the new United States weren't allowed to vote. They had no say about who was in charge and who made the laws. That included African Americans forced into slavery, who had no freedoms. It included Native Americans, who had settled the continent long before the new

Americans arrived, and were being pushed off their lands. It included women. It included immigrants and workers and poor people, who were treated very badly by their bosses. In most places, these people didn't have the right to vote. The only people who could vote were white men who owned propery— like horses and farms.

Today, if you're an American citizen and at least eighteen years old, you can vote, and when you vote, your ballot is kept a secret.

If "all men are created equal" as the Declaration said, then shouldn't we all have the same rights and freedoms? And what about women? Slowly, over the next two hundred years, men and women from all walks of life would struggle for and gain those rights. We're a more free and fair country today thanks to their efforts.

Elizabeth Freeman, who was forced to be a slave, knew that she deserved to be free. Just four years after the Declaration of Independence was signed, she got a judge to listen to her case—that she was "created equal" like the Declaration said—and she won! This case helped the state of Massachusetts eventually end slavery, but it would take a long time before slavery was ended in all of the states.

HOW COULD THERE BE SLAVERY IN THE "LAND OF THE FREE"?

It's hard for many of us to imagine today that slavery was once a way of life here in America. If you had been born enslaved, you would have been taken away from your parents as a young child and forced against your will to work for no pay. Slave owners could sell you anytime they chose to a large faraway farm, or plantation, the same way they would sell an ox or a mule—and you simply couldn't choose where you lived or how you spent your time.

Most enslaved children didn't have many clothes, shoes, or a real bed to sleep in and never even knew their birthdays. No one would've been allowed to teach you to read or write, and you could be badly beaten if you tried to escape.

Sadly, many of our nation's founders—including Thomas Jefferson and George Washington—enslaved people. Slave owners lived comfortable lives in large homes, with fancy clothes and lots of food, all because of the hard work they forced enslaved people to do.

Even so, all sorts of people in America realized that slavery was wrong, and they tried to get our leaders to end it. These people were called abolition- ists. Over time, Northern states outlawed slavery, so enslaved people in the South risked their lives to escape to freedom in the North.

Thousands of enslaved people bravely escaped through the Underground Railroad. It wasn't an actual railroad with train tracks and cars, but a secret trail of friendly white and black people who wanted to help enslaved people reach freedom. Escaped slaves and their helpers would find ways to send messages to one another and come up with safe passage routes to freedom.

Harriet Tubman, heroine of American freedom, was one of the great "conductors" on the Underground Railroad. After she escaped from slavery, she bravely returned to the South many more times, outsmarting slave hunters who tried to capture her. In the end, she helped as many as three hundred enslaved people escape to freedom!

Henry "Box" Brown was born enslaved in Virginia. He was determined to escape when his wife and children were sold to a plantation far away in North Carolina. He came up with an ingenious plan—to be shipped in a box to Philadelphia, where he could be free—and it worked! He went public with his story and for years taught about the importance of freeing enslaved people.

HOW WERE ALL THE ENSLAVED PEOPLE FINALLY FREED?

Ultimately, it took a terrible war and a great president to end slavery in America once and for all.

Abraham Lincoln was against slavery, but the Southern states wanted to keep it. So when Lincoln was elected president in 1860, the Southern slave states started their own separate government—the Confederacy—so they could continue enslaving people. Lincoln was committed to keeping America—the Union—one whole country. This is how America's Civil War between the North and the South began.

It was a long, bitter war where even brothers

from the same family battled against each other. During the war, President Lincoln signed the Emancipation Proclamation, which freed enslaved people in Confederate states. Emancipation is another word for freedom. As Union soldiers marched through the South, they carried copies of the Emancipation Proclamation to show Southern slave owners that they had to free their enslaved people. Many of these newly freed slaves joined the Union's fight. Finally, when the war was over, all

the enslaved people in America were freed and the Union was saved!

During and after Lincoln's presidency, the circle of American freedom grew wider to include more people with three new amendments to the Constitution. The Thirteenth Amendment to the Constitution ended slavery in America once and for all. The next two amendments promised citizenship to anyone born in America, including former slaves, and gave African American men the right to vote.

Sojourner Truth, a courageous escaped slave, criss-crossed the country collecting supplies for black Union soldiers and speaking out against slavery and for the right of women to vote. Today, she's honored with her very own statue at the US Capitol in Washington, DC.

SOJOURNER TRUTH

One of America's greatest leaders was the abolitionist Frederick Douglass. After the enslaved people were freed, he kept up the fight for the civil rights of African Americans, especially trying to get the right to vote for formerly enslaved people. The Fifteenth Amendment to the Constitution granted African American men the right to vote.

HOW DID WOMEN GET THE RIGHT TO VOTE?

Many laws didn't treat women the same as men, but because they weren't allowed to vote, women had a very hard time changing those rules.

When Elizabeth Cady Stanton and Lucretia Mott were excluded from an important meeting just because they were women, they knew that things had to change. So in 1848, they used their First Amendment rights and gathered a brave group of women (along with a few men) in Seneca Falls, New York, to produce their own declaration starting with a small but important addition: "that all men *and women* are created equal." They demanded that women receive the same rights and opportunities as men, including the right to vote.

For years, women organized and assembled, picketed, protested, and even got locked up in jail fighting for their rights. Finally, in 1920, nearly 150 years after the Declaration of Independence was written, women won the right to vote!

Still, it would take many more years of struggle and hard work before all American citizens could actually use their voting rights.

Can you imagine living at a time or in a state where your mom couldn't open her own bank account? Or your sister wasn't allowed to go to college? Getting the right to vote helped women to change unfair laws.

Women struggled for the vote from the very start of our country. Abigail Adams—the wife of America's second president, John Adams, and the mother of our sixth president, John Quincy Adams—compared women to the colonists who were trying to overthrow the bully king of England. She asked why women should be "bound by any Laws in which we have no voice."

Even though women weren't allowed to vote, nothing would stop Susan B. Anthony from trying, because she believed that failure was impossible. In 1872, she and fourteen other women went ahead and voted at their local polling station, and Susan was arrested! The Nineteenth Amendment, granting women the vote, is named after her.

WHO IS AN AMERICAN CITIZEN?

Anyone who is born in America is automatically a citizen. But you can become a citizen if you weren't born here.

Immigrants aren't born here; they come from other countries. And America is very popular—more immigrants from around the world flock here, to the "land of the free," than to any other country.

America has always been a country of immigrants, who brought their cultures with them—different foods, religions, and languages—and helped shape the America we know today. Back in America's early days, colonists came here from England so they could practice their religion freely and maybe get a chance to own a farm or start a business.

But when tens of millions of new immigrants started streaming into America around one hundred years after the Declaration was signed, some Americans didn't want to allow the new arrivals to vote.

Slowly, over the course of many decades, we changed the laws to be more welcoming. Today, immigrants can become American citizens so that they can enjoy American freedoms like the right to vote. But still, not every citizen gets to vote. Like who? Well, kids like you!

Sometimes the journey to America took several weeks on packed ships sailing stormy seas where passengers would get seasick or worse. But when they finally neared New York City, immigrants felt hopeful as they imagined their new lives in America. "Mothers and fathers lifted up babies so [that] they too could see . . . the Statue of Liberty," one immigrant remembered.

Thousands of men who came from China helped build the Transcontinental Railroad, which spanned America's broad middle, covering 3,000 miles. Workers had to blast tunnels through huge mountains and scale cliffs to lay track—but the Chinese workers brought special expertise that they had learned from their home country. It would take eighty years before Chinese immigrants were allowed to become American citizens.

WHAT RIGHTS AND FREEDOMS DO CHILDREN HAVE?

Do you like going to school? It's a tough question, right? You probably love seeing your friends every day, but maybe you don't like the school lunch. Or maybe you love everything about school but you still look forward to vacations, when you don't have to worry about homework or waking up early.

If you can believe it, making sure that every kid gets the chance to go to school is one of the most important freedoms we have. Why? Because about one hundred years ago in America, many young children had jobs where they had to work very hard for long hours and very little pay.

Often children were used for dangerous jobs specifically because they were small. Sometimes they sorted through heaps of coal speeding down chutes, which would make their hands bleed, or cleaned the insides of dangerous machines with fast-spinning parts that could badly injure them.

Kids didn't have much time to play or learn; they weren't free to be kids. Nowadays, we have laws to protect most kids from having to do very hard jobs, and all kids get to go to school. Work hours are limited for older kids, and there are laws saying that people have to be paid a fair amount for their work.

Mother Jones, who spoke out against child labor, led child workers on a 125-mile march—all the way from Philadelphia to New York—to show the world that children should be free to be kids. Some of the kids had been injured at work and many were hungry and tired from their hard jobs, but they proudly held signs demanding more time to go to school.

A strike is when workers use their freedom to assemble to join together and refuse to work until they get treated fairly—which means better pay and safer working conditions. When Clara Lemlich was twenty-three years old, she famously led a huge strike called the "the Uprising of the 20,000"—mostly young women workers!

WHAT DOES FREEDOM HAVE TO DO WITH YOUR JOB?

What do you want to be when you grow up? Maybe a scientist? Or a police officer? Or maybe a dancer? Whatever job you choose, you deserve to get paid enough to have the freedom to buy food, clothes, and medicine to keep your family healthy and to have a home in a safe neighborhood. You also deserve to work enough hours to make a living, but not so many that you don't have the chance to enjoy free time with your family too.

Too much work can be hard on a family, but so can too little. When grown-ups lose their jobs, life can get even tougher. That's what happened in 1929 when the Great Depression hit. During this time, banks and schools closed and farmlands dried out because the rains would not come. Moms, dads, and teenagers lost their jobs and their families suffered—they were hungry and homeless. Without school or work, millions of people had to leave their homes behind.

Even though it was against the rules, kids hopped onto trains and rode the rails during the Great Depression— some because their parents didn't have enough money to support them anymore, others because schools had closed and they went looking for work wherever they could find it. But life on the road was dangerous, nights were cold, and kids often went days without food.

When Franklin Roosevelt became president in 1933, he started programs and signed laws to help people get back to work. Years later, he called this "freedom from want"—freedom from being too poor or homeless or hungry—because there are basics that all people need and deserve. People still fall on hard times today, but it would happen a lot more if President Roosevelt hadn't helped during

the Great Depression and put in place laws that protect people even today.

One of President Roosevelt's new programs gave hundreds of thousands of young people jobs building and maintaining national and state parks all around the country. You can think of them the next time you dive into a pool, hike a trail, or cool off under a shady tree at one of your favorite parks!

WITH "FREEDOM FROM WANT," WAS AMERICA TRULY THE "LAND OF THE FREE"?

No, it wasn't. That's because "Jim Crow" laws bullied African Americans and forced them to stay separated—or segregated—from white people. Some laws made African Americans drink out of separate water fountains or sit in the backs of city buses. How can you be free if you aren't allowed to sit in any open seat on the bus or if a restaurant refuses to serve you just because of the color of your skin?

Other laws stopped African Americans from voting. They used tricky reading tests or required very poor people to pay money to vote, which they couldn't afford.

To fight these unfair and cruel laws, Dr. Martin Luther King Jr., the great leader of the civil rights movement, inspired African Americans to peacefully protest—gather together for marches, songs, and boycotts—so that all of us would be treated the same.

Dr. King famously said, "I have a dream that my four little children will one day live in a nation where they will not be judged by the color of their skin but by the content of their character." Shouldn't we all be judged by who we are, not by how we look?

Brave African Americans all over the country protested peacefully against unfair treatment. When Claudette Colvin was fifteen years old, she refused to give up her seat on a bus and was arrested and sent to jail. Nine months later, a grown-up civil rights activist, Rosa Parks, would do the same thing and start the Montgomery Bus Boycott to show the world how harsh and unfair these laws were.

After many years of long, hard struggles, they succeeded! New laws passed stating that African Americans—or anyone else—couldn't be treated worse or kept from voting just because of the color of their skin. One hundred years after emancipation from slavery, millions more Americans were free at last!

One way civil rights activists protested peacefully was through "sit-ins" at restaurants that refused to serve African Americans. One sit-in began with four young African American men refusing to give up their seats at a "whites-only" lunch counter. By the sixth day, one thousand students showed up to protest, and by the end of the next month, there were sit-ins in fifty-five cities around the country!

Throughout the South, white and black children attended separate schools, but the schools for white children had better playgrounds, books, and other supplies. When new laws finally allowed black and white kids to attend the same school, the change wasn't so easy. Brave Ruby Bridges was six years old when she was the only African American to attend an all-white school in New Orleans. Federal marshals had to protect her at school for a whole year, and she spent most of her time alone because her white classmates' families wouldn't send their kids to class with her.

HOW CAN WE KEEP SPREADING AND CELEBRATING AMERICAN FREEDOM?

Imagine singing a song by yourself. The melody might be clear, but no one can hear you from far away. As more and more friends and neighbors join you, the song gets louder until your voices can be heard far and wide.

That's kind of how freedom has grown in America. The original tunes—the Declaration of Independence, the Constitution, and the Bill of Rights—were right on key, but too few people could enjoy the freedoms described in them, so the song was too quiet. But the tune did get stuck in a lot of people's heads, and as they started to sing along, to join their voices in the trials and triumphs of freedom, the choir grew louder until the song could be heard around the world. Our growing freedom here inspires people all over the world to know that their voices matter.

But the song isn't over yet, and anyone can join this choir, no matter how young or old you are! As you look around your neighborhood, as you learn more about the world from your teachers and parents and the news, do you think all people have the same freedoms that you do? How can you use your voice to make America more fair and free?

Americans have always cared about freedom—in our own country and around the world. Our brave soldiers have gone to different countries to help other people fight for freedom. Would you fight for someone else's freedom?

Voting is a big deal. When you turn eighteen, you'll have the chance to vote and make America stronger and more free and fair. How will you celebrate your new freedom? If you were born in another country, will you try to become a US citizen?

TIMELINE

1776 Declaration of Independence written: proclaimed America's independence from England and that all men are created equal

1787 Constitution written: established the supreme law of the land

1788 Constitution ratified: delegates voted to approve the Constitution

1791 Bill of Rights ratified: established rights that no government could take away from the people

1848 Declaration of Sentiments presented: said that all men and women are created equal

1863 Emancipation Proclamation issued: declared that slaves in Confederate states must be freed

1865 Thirteenth Amendment to the Constitution ratified: outlawed slavery

1868 Fourteenth Amendment to the Constitution ratified: granted citizenship to former slaves

1870 Fifteenth Amendment to the Constitution ratified: granted African American men the right to vote

1920 Nineteenth Amendment to the Constitution ratified: granted women the right to vote

1924 Indian Citizenship Act signed: granted American citizenship to Native Americans

1935 National Labor Relations Act signed: said workers could band together to negotiate for fair wages and better treatment

1935 Social Security Act signed: set up a program to provide money for the elderly and others in need

1938 Fair Labor Standards Act signed: said people had to be paid enough money for their hard work and didn't have to work more than eight hours each day, and banned child labor

1954 *Brown v. Board of Education*: the Supreme Court said that children could not be segregated in schools based on their race

1964 Civil Rights Act signed: outlawed segregation and race-based discrimination

1965 Voting Rights Act signed: outlawed tricks and shams that stopped citizens from voting

1965 Immigration and Nationality Act signed: said that immigrants from any country were welcome in America and that immigrant families should be allowed to stay together

1971 Twenty-Sixth Amendment ratified: granted citizens eighteen years and older the right to vote

2015 Marriage equality upheld: legalized right of same-sex couples to marry

WHO'S WHO

Below, you'll find the names of some of the great leaders in this book, in order of appearance, who made America more free. Will you be America's next great freedom leader?

President Thomas Jefferson

Robert Hemings

John Hancock

Benjamin Franklin

Elizabeth Freeman

President George Washington

Harriet Tubman

Henry "Box" Brown

President Abraham Lincoln

Sojourner Truth

Frederick Douglass

Elizabeth Cady Stanton

Lucretia Mott

Abigail Adams

President John Adams

Susan B. Anthony

Clara Lemlich

Mother Jones

President Franklin Delano
    Roosevelt

Dr. Martin Luther King Jr.

Claudette Colvin

Rosa Parks

Ruby Bridges

AUTHOR'S NOTE

The interplay among freedom and justice and rights has animated the evolution of American social progress from our earliest days through today. Our history has been a dynamic push-and-pull between freedom and responsibility; between the rights of different groups of people; between government power and civil liberties; and between the various levels and branches of government. In a seeming paradox, freedom in America has only expanded through the rule of law—laws that abolished slavery, enfranchised all citizens, expanded the rights of children, workers, immigrants, and minorities. Generations of Americans used the founding documents as templates to broaden access to freedom for those who were excluded from their promises. We still have barriers in America's path toward an ever "more perfect union," but I hope this book gives readers a sense that they can effect change like the inspirational leaders mentioned in its pages and that progress is possible because justice is woven into the very founding fibers of this country.

In addition to poring over primary sources including the Constitution, the Bill of Rights, the Declaration of Independence, and pivotal documents, speeches, and laws (often through the National Archives at archives.gov), below are some of the excellent books I used as references.

★ *Kids on Strike!* by Susan Campbell Bartoletti
★ *Journeys for Freedom: A New Look at America's Story*, by Susan Buckley (Author), Elspeth Leacock (Author), Rodica Prato (Illustrator)
★ *Liberty's Children: Stories of Eleven Revolutionary War Children*, by Scotti McAuliff Cohn
★ *Give Me Liberty! An American History*, by Eric Foner

- ★ *The Story of American Freedom*, by Eric Foner
- ★ *Freedom Walkers: The Story of the Montgomery Bus Boycott*, by Russell Freedman
- ★ *Immigrant Kids*, by Russell Freedman
- ★ *Shhh! We're Writing the Constitution!* by Jean Fritz, drawings by Tomie dePaola
- ★ *North Star to Freedom: The Story of the Underground Railroad*, by Gena K. Gorrell
- ★ *We Were There, Too! Young People in US History*, by Phillip Hoose
- ★ *If You Were There When They Signed the Constitution*, by Elizabeth Levy, illustrated by Joan Holub
- ★ *Marching for Freedom: Walk Together Children and Don't You Grow Weary*, by Elizabeth Partridge
- ★ *The Fight to Vote*, by Michael Waldman
- ★ *One Woman One Vote: Rediscovering the Women's Suffrage Movement*, by Marjorie Spruill Wheeler (Editor)

Don't miss the other fun and fact-filled books in this series!

WHAT'S THE BIG DEAL ABOUT
First Ladies

Ruby Shamir   Matt Faulkner

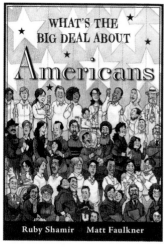

WHAT'S THE BIG DEAL ABOUT
Americans

Ruby Shamir   Matt Faulkner

WHAT'S THE BIG DEAL ABOUT
Elections

VOTE

Ruby Shamir   Matt Faulkner